NATURE LOVE

NITESH SINWAL

Contents

CHAPTER ONE

Nature

For other uses, see Nature (disambiguation).

"Natural" redirects here. For other uses, see Natural (disambiguation).

Shaki Waterfall, Armenia

Bachalpsee in the Swiss Alps

A winter landscape in Lapland, Finland

Lightning strikes during the eruption of the Galunggung volcano, West Java, in 1982

Life in the abyssal oceans

South Penghu Marine National Park of Taiwan, showing the wonder of nature

Nature, in the broadest sense, is the physical world or universe. "Nature" can refer to the phenomena of the physical world, and also to life in general. The study of nature is a large, if not the only, part of science. Although humans are part of nature, human activity is often understood as a separate category from other natural phenomena.[1]

The word nature is borrowed from the Old French nature and is derived from the Latin word natura, or "essential qualities, innate disposition", and in ancient times, literally meant "birth".[2] In ancient philosophy, natura is mostly used as the Latin translation of the Greek word physis (φύσις), which originally related to the intrinsic characteristics of plants, animals, and other features of the world to develop of their own accord.[3][4] The concept of nature as a whole, the physical universe, is one of several expansions of the original notion;[1] it began with certain core applications of the word φύσις by pre-Socratic philosophers (though this word had a dynamic dimension then, especially for Heraclitus), and has steadily gained currency ever since.

During the advent of modern scientific method in the last several centuries, nature became the passive reality, organized and moved by divine laws.[5][6] With the Industrial revolution, nature increasingly became seen as the part of reality deprived from intentional intervention: it was hence considered as sacred by some traditions (Rousseau, American transcendentalism) or a mere decorum for divine providence or human history (Hegel, Marx). However, a vitalist vision of nature, closer to the presocratic one, got reborn at the same time, especially after Charles Darwin.[1]

Within the various uses of the word today, "nature" often refers to geology and wildlife. Nature can refer to the general realm of living plants and animals, and in some cases to the processes associated with inanimate objects—the way that particular types of things exist and change of their own accord, such as the weather and geology of the Earth. It is often taken to mean the "natural environment" or wilderness—wild animals, rocks, forest, and in general those things that have not been substantially altered by human intervention, or which persist despite human intervention. For example, manufactured objects and human interaction generally are not considered part of nature, unless qualified as, for example, "human nature" or "the whole of nature". This more traditional concept of natural things that can still be found today implies a distinction between the natural and the artificial, with the artificial being understood as that which has been brought into being by a human consciousness or a human mind. Depending on the particular context, the term "natural" might also be distinguished from the unnatural or the supernatural.[1]

Earth is the only planet known to support life, and its natural features are the subject of many fields of scientific research. Within the Solar System, it is third closest to the Sun; it is the largest terrestrial planet and the fifth largest overall. Its most prominent climatic features are its two large polar regions, two relatively narrow temperate zones, and a wide equatorial tropical to subtropical region.[7] Precipitation varies widely with location, from several metres of water per year to less than a millimetre. 71 percent of the Earth's surface is covered by salt-water oceans. The remainder consists of continents and islands, with most of the inhabited land in the Northern Hemisphere.

Earth has evolved through geological and biological processes that have left traces of the original conditions. The outer surface is divided into several gradually migrating tectonic plates. The interior remains active, with a thick layer of plastic mantle and an iron-filled core that generates a magnetic field. This iron core is composed of a solid inner phase, and a fluid outer phase. Convective motion in the core generates electric currents through dynamo action, and these, in turn, generate the geomagnetic field.

The atmospheric conditions have been significantly altered from the original conditions by the presence of life-forms,[8] which create an ecological balance that stabilizes the surface conditions. Despite the wide regional variations in climate by latitude and other geographic factors, the long-term average global climate is quite stable during interglacial periods,[9] and variations of a degree or two of average global temperature have historically had major effects on the ecological balance, and on the actual geography of the Earth.[10][11]

Geology

Main article: Geology

Geology is the science and study of the solid and liquid matter that constitutes the Earth. The field of geology encompasses the study of the composition, structure, physical properties, dynamics, and history of Earth materials, and the processes by which they are formed, moved, and changed. The field is a major academic discipline, and is also important for mineral and hydrocarbon extraction, knowledge about and mitigation of natural hazards, some Geotechnical engineering fields, and understanding past climates and environments.

Geological evolution

Three types of geological plate tectonic boundaries

The geology of an area evolves through time as rock units are deposited and inserted and deformational processes change their shapes and locations.

Rock units are first emplaced either by deposition onto the surface or intrude into the overlying rock. Deposition can occur when sediments settle onto the surface of the Earth and later lithify into sedimentary rock, or when as volcanic material such as volcanic ash or lava flows, blanket the surface. Igneous intrusions such as batholiths, laccoliths, dikes, and sills, push upwards into the overlying rock, and crystallize as they intrude.

After the initial sequence of rocks has been deposited, the rock units can be deformed and/or metamorphosed. Deformation typically occurs as a result of horizontal shortening, horizontal extension, or side-to-side (strike-slip) motion. These structural regimes broadly relate to convergent boundaries, divergent boundaries, and transform boundaries, respectively, between tectonic plates.

Historical perspective

Main articles: History of the Earth and Evolution

An animation showing the movement of the continents from the separation of Pangaea until the present day

Earth is estimated to have formed 4.54 billion years ago from the solar nebula, along with the Sun and other planets.[12] The Moon formed roughly 20 million years later. Initially molten, the outer layer of the Earth cooled, resulting in the solid crust. Outgassing and volcanic activity produced the primordial atmosphere. Condensing water vapor, most or all of which came from ice delivered by comets, produced the oceans and other water sources.[13] The highly energetic chemistry is believed to have produced a self-replicating molecule around 4 billion years ago.[14]

Plankton inhabit oceans, seas and lakes, and have existed in various forms for at least 2 billion years[15]

Continents formed, then broke up and reformed as the surface of Earth reshaped over hundreds of millions of years, occasionally combining to make a supercontinent. Roughly 750 million years ago, the earliest known supercontinent Rodinia, began to break apart. The continents later recombined to form Pannotia which broke apart about 540 million years ago, then finally Pangaea, which broke apart about 180 million years ago.[16]

During the Neoproterozoic era, freezing temperatures covered much of the Earth in glaciers and ice sheets. This hypothesis has been termed the "Snowball Earth", and it is of particular interest as it precedes the Cambrian explosion in which multicellular life forms began to proliferate about 530–540 million years ago.[17]

Since the Cambrian explosion there have been five distinctly identifiable mass extinctions.[18] The last mass extinction occurred some 66 million years ago, when a meteorite collision probably triggered the extinction of the non-avian dinosaurs and other large reptiles, but spared small animals such as mammals. Over the past 66 million years, mammalian life diversified.[19]

Several million years ago, a species of small African ape gained the ability to stand upright.[15] The subsequent advent of human life, and the development of agriculture and further civilization allowed humans to affect the Earth more rapidly than any previous life form, affecting both the nature and quantity of other organisms as well as global climate. By comparison, the Great Oxygenation Event, produced by the proliferation of algae during the Siderian period, required about 300 million years to culminate.

The present era is classified as part of a mass extinction event, the Holocene extinction event, the fastest ever to have occurred.[20][21] Some, such as E. O. Wilson of Harvard University, predict that human destruction of the biosphere could cause the extinction of one-half of all species in the next 100 years.[22] The extent of the current extinction event is still being researched, debated and calculated by biologists.[23][24][25]

Atmosphere, climate, and weather

Blue light is scattered more than other wavelengths by the gases in the atmosphere, giving the Earth a blue halo when seen from space

Main articles: Atmosphere of Earth, Climate, and Weather

The Earth's atmosphere is a key factor in sustaining the ecosystem. The thin layer of gases that envelops the Earth is held in place by gravity. Air is mostly nitrogen, oxygen, water vapor, with much smaller amounts of carbon dioxide, argon, etc. The atmospheric pressure declines steadily with altitude. The ozone layer plays an important role in depleting the amount of ultraviolet (UV) radiation that reaches the surface. As DNA is readily damaged by UV light, this serves to protect life at the surface. The atmosphere also retains heat during the night, thereby reducing the daily temperature extremes.

Terrestrial weather occurs almost exclusively in the lower part of the atmosphere, and serves as a convective system for redistributing heat.[26] Ocean currents are another important factor in determining climate, particularly the major underwater thermohaline circulation which distributes heat energy from the equatorial oceans to the polar regions. These currents help to moderate the differences in temperature between winter and summer in the temperate zones. Also, without the redistributions of heat energy by the ocean currents and atmosphere, the tropics would be much hotter, and the polar regions much colder.

Lightning

Weather can have both beneficial and harmful effects. Extremes in weather, such as tornadoes or hurricanes and cyclones, can expend large amounts of energy along their paths, and produce devastation. Surface vegetation has evolved a dependence on the seasonal variation of the weather, and sudden changes lasting only a few years can have a dramatic effect, both on the vegetation and on the animals which depend on its growth for their food.

Climate is a measure of the long-term trends in the weather. Various factors are known to influence the climate, including ocean currents, surface albedo, greenhouse gases, variations in the solar luminosity, and changes to the Earth's orbit. Based on historical records, the Earth is known to have undergone drastic climate changes in the past, including ice ages.

A tornado in central Oklahoma

The climate of a region depends on a number of factors, especially latitude. A latitudinal band of the surface with similar climatic attributes forms a climate region. There are a number of such regions, ranging from the tropical climate at the equator to the polar climate in the northern and southern extremes. Weather is also influenced by the seasons, which result from the Earth's axis being tilted relative to its orbital plane. Thus, at any given time during the summer or winter, one part of the Earth is more directly exposed to the rays of the sun. This exposure alternates as the Earth revolves in its orbit. At any given time, regardless of season, the northern and southern hemispheres experience opposite seasons.

Weather is a chaotic system that is readily modified by small changes to the environment, so accurate weather forecasting is limited to only a few days.[27] Overall, two things are happening worldwide: (1) temperature is increasing on the average; and (2) regional climates have been undergoing noticeable changes.[28]

Water on the Earth

The Iguazu Falls on the border between Brazil and Argentina

Main article: Water

Water is a chemical substance that is composed of hydrogen and oxygen (H2O) and is vital for all known forms of life.[29] In typical usage, water refers only to its liquid form or state, but the substance also has a solid state, ice, and a gaseous state, water vapor, or steam. Water covers 71% of the Earth's surface.[30] On Earth, it is found mostly in oceans and other large bodies of water, with 1.6% of water below ground in aquifers and 0.001% in the air as vapor, clouds, and precipitation.[31][32] Oceans hold 97% of surface water, glaciers, and polar ice caps 2.4%, and other land surface water such as rivers, lakes, and ponds 0.6%. Additionally, a minute amount of the Earth's water is contained within biological bodies and manufactured products.

Oceans

A view of the Atlantic Ocean from Leblon, Rio de Janeiro

Main article: Ocean

An ocean is a major body of saline water, and a principal component of the hydrosphere. Approximately 71% of the Earth's surface (an area of some 361 million square kilometers) is covered by ocean, a continuous body of water that is customarily divided into several principal oceans and smaller seas. More than half of this area is over 3,000 meters (9,800 feet) deep. Average oceanic salinity is around 35 parts per thousand (ppt) (3.5%), and nearly all seawater has a salinity in the range of 30 to 38 ppt. Though generally recognized as several 'separate' oceans, these waters comprise one global, interconnected body of salt water often referred to as the World Ocean or global ocean.[33][34] This concept of a global ocean as a continuous body of water with relatively free interchange among its parts is of fundamental importance to oceanography.[35]

The major oceanic divisions are defined in part by the continents, various archipelagos, and other criteria: these divisions are (in descending order of size) the Pacific Ocean, the Atlantic Ocean, the Indian Ocean, the Southern Ocean, and the Arctic Ocean. Smaller regions of the oceans are called seas, gulfs, bays and other names. There are also salt lakes, which are smaller bodies of landlocked saltwater that are not interconnected with the World Ocean. Two notable examples of salt lakes are the Aral Sea and the Great Salt Lake.

Lakes

Lake Mapourika, New Zealand

Main article: Lake

A lake (from Latin word lacus) is a terrain feature (or physical feature), a body of liquid on the surface of a world that is localized to the bottom of basin (another type of landform or terrain feature; that is, it is not global) and moves slowly if it moves at all. On Earth, a body of water is considered a lake when it is inland, not part of the ocean, is larger and deeper than a pond, and is fed by a river.[36][37] The only world other than Earth known to harbor lakes is Titan, Saturn's largest moon, which has lakes of ethane, most likely mixed with methane. It is not known if Titan's lakes are fed by rivers, though Titan's surface is carved by numerous river beds. Natural lakes on Earth are generally found in mountainous areas, rift zones, and areas with ongoing or recent glaciation. Other lakes are found in endorheic basins or along the courses of mature rivers. In some parts of the world, there are many lakes because of chaotic drainage patterns left over from the last ice age. All lakes are temporary over geologic time scales, as they will slowly fill in with sediments or spill out of the basin containing them.

Ponds

The Westborough Reservoir (Mill Pond) in Westborough, Massachusetts

Main article: Pond

A pond is a body of standing water, either natural or man-made, that is usually smaller than a lake. A wide variety of man-made bodies of water are classified as ponds, including water gardens designed for aesthetic ornamentation, fish ponds designed for commercial fish breeding, and solar ponds designed to store thermal energy. Ponds and lakes are distinguished from streams via current speed. While currents in streams are easily observed, ponds and lakes possess thermally driven micro-currents and moderate wind driven currents. These features distinguish a pond from many other aquatic terrain features, such as stream pools and tide pools.

Rivers

The Nile river in Cairo, Egypt's capital city

Main article: River

A river is a natural watercourse,[38] usually freshwater, flowing towards an ocean, a lake, a sea or another river. In a few cases, a river simply flows into the ground or dries up completely before reaching another body of water. Small rivers may also be called by several other names, including stream, creek, brook, rivulet, and rill; there is no general rule that defines what can be called a river. Many names for small rivers are specific to geographic location; one example is Burn in Scotland and North-east England. Sometimes a river is said to be larger than a creek, but this is not always the case, due to vagueness in the language.[39] A river is part of the hydrological cycle. Water within a river is generally collected from precipitation through surface runoff, groundwater recharge, springs, and the release of stored water in natural ice and snowpacks (i.e., from glaciers).

Streams

A rocky stream in Hawaii

Main article: Stream

A stream is a flowing body of water with a current, confined within a bed and stream banks. In the United States, a stream is classified as a watercourse less than 60 feet (18 metres) wide. Streams are important as conduits in the water cycle, instruments in groundwater recharge, and they serve as corridors for fish and wildlife migration. The biological habitat in the immediate vicinity of a stream is called a riparian zone. Given the status of the ongoing Holocene extinction, streams play an important corridor role in connecting fragmented habitats and thus in conserving biodiversity. The study of streams and waterways in general involves many branches of inter-disciplinary natural science and engineering, including hydrology, fluvial geomorphology, aquatic ecology, fish biology, riparian ecology, and others.

Ecosystems

Loch Lomond in Scotland forms a relatively isolated ecosystem. The fish community of this lake has remained unchanged over a very long period of time.[40]

Lush green Aravalli Mountain Range in the Desert country – Rajasthan, India. A wonder how such greenery can exist in hot Rajasthan, a place well known for its Thar Desert

An aerial view of a human ecosystem. Pictured is the city of Chicago

Main articles: Ecology and Ecosystem

Ecosystems are composed of a variety of biotic and abiotic components that function in an interrelated way.[41] The structure and composition is determined by various environmental factors that are interrelated. Variations of these factors will initiate dynamic modifications to the ecosystem. Some of the more important components are soil, atmosphere, radiation from the sun, water, and living organisms.

Peñas Blancas, part of the Bosawás Biosphere Reserve. Located northeast of the city of Jinotega in Northeastern Nicaragua

Central to the ecosystem concept is the idea that living organisms interact with every other element in their local environment. Eugene Odum, a founder of ecology, stated: "Any unit that includes all of the organisms (ie: the "community") in a given area interacting with the physical environment so that a flow of energy leads to clearly defined trophic structure, biotic diversity, and material cycles (i.e.: exchange of materials between living and nonliving parts) within the system is an ecosystem."[42] Within the ecosystem, species are connected and dependent upon one another in the food chain, and exchange energy and matter between themselves as well as with their environment.[43] The human ecosystem concept is based on the human/nature dichotomy and the idea that all species are ecologically dependent on each other, as well as with the abiotic constituents of their biotope.[44]

A smaller unit of size is called a microecosystem. For example, a microsystem can be a stone and all the life under it. A macroecosystem might involve a whole ecoregion, with its drainage basin.[45]

Wilderness

Old growth European Beech forest in Biogradska Gora National Park, Montenegro

Main article: Wilderness

Wilderness is generally defined as areas that have not been significantly modified by human activity. Wilderness areas can be found in preserves, estates, farms, conservation preserves, ranches, national forests, national parks, and even in urban areas along rivers, gulches, or otherwise undeveloped areas. Wilderness areas and protected parks are considered important for the survival of certain species, ecological studies, conservation, and solitude. Some nature writers believe wilderness areas are vital for the human spirit and creativity,[46] and some ecologists consider wilderness areas to be an integral part of the Earth's self-sustaining natural ecosystem (the biosphere). They may also preserve historic genetic traits and that they provide habitat for wild flora and fauna that may be difficult or impossible to recreate in zoos, arboretums, or laboratories.

Life

CHAPTER TWO

Aesthetics and beauty

Aesthetics and beauty

Aesthetically pleasing flowers

Beauty in nature has historically been a prevalent theme in art and books, filling large sections of libraries and bookstores. That nature has been depicted and celebrated by so much art, photography, poetry, and other literature shows the strength with which many people associate nature and beauty. Reasons why this association exists, and what the association consists of, are studied by the branch of philosophy called aesthetics. Beyond certain basic characteristics that many philosophers agree about to explain what is seen as beautiful, the opinions are virtually endless.[87] Nature and wildness have been important subjects in various eras of world history. An early tradition of landscape art began in China during the Tang Dynasty (618–907). The tradition of representing nature as it is became one of the aims of Chinese painting and was a significant influence in Asian art.

Although natural wonders are celebrated in the Psalms and the Book of Job, wilderness portrayals in art became more prevalent in the 1800s, especially in the works of the Romantic movement. British artists John Constable and J. M. W. Turner turned their attention to capturing the beauty of the natural world in their paintings. Before that, paintings had been primarily of religious scenes or of human beings. William Wordsworth's poetry described the wonder of the natural world, which had formerly been viewed as a threatening place. Increasingly the valuing of nature became an aspect of Western culture.[88] This artistic movement also coincided with the Transcendentalist movement in the Western world. A common classical idea of beautiful art involves the word mimesis, the imitation of nature. Also in the realm of ideas about beauty in nature is that the perfect is implied through perfect mathematical forms and more generally by patterns in nature. As David Rothenburg writes, "The beautiful is the root of science and the goal of art, the highest possibility that humanity can ever hope to see".[89]:281

Matter and energy

The first few hydrogen atom electron orbitals shown as cross-sections with color-coded probability density

Main articles: Matter and Energy

Some fields of science see nature as matter in motion, obeying certain laws of nature which science seeks to understand. For this reason the most fundamental science is generally understood to be "physics"—the name for which is still recognizable as meaning that it is the "study of nature".

Matter is commonly defined as the substance of which physical objects are composed. It constitutes the observable universe. The visible components of the universe are now believed to compose only 4.9 percent of the total mass. The remainder is believed to consist of 26.8 percent cold dark matter and 68.3 percent dark energy.[90] The exact arrangement of these components is still unknown and is under intensive investigation by physicists.

The behaviour of matter and energy throughout the observable universe appears to follow well-defined physical laws. These laws have been employed to produce cosmological models that successfully explain the structure and the evolution of the universe we can observe. The mathematical expressions of the laws of physics employ a set of twenty physical constants[91] that appear to be static across the observable universe.[92] The values of these constants have been carefully measured, but the reason for their specific values remains a mystery.

Beyond Earth

Main articles: Outer space, Universe, and Extraterrestrial life

Planets of the Solar System (Sizes to scale, distances and illumination not to scale)

NGC 4414 is a spiral galaxy in the constellation Coma Berenices about 56,000 light-years in diameter and approximately 60 million light-years from Earth

Outer space, also simply called space, refers to the relatively empty regions of the Universe outside the atmospheres of celestial bodies. Outer space is used to distinguish it from airspace (and terrestrial locations). There is no discrete boundary between Earth's atmosphere and space, as the atmosphere gradually attenuates with increasing altitude. Outer space within the Solar System is called interplanetary space, which passes over into interstellar space at what is known as the heliopause.

Outer space is sparsely filled with several dozen types of organic molecules discovered to date by microwave spectroscopy, blackbody radiation left over from the Big Bang and the origin of the universe, and cosmic rays, which include ionized atomic nuclei and various subatomic particles. There is also some gas, plasma and dust, and small meteors. Additionally, there are signs of human life in outer space today, such as material left over from previous crewed and uncrewed launches which are a potential hazard to spacecraft. Some of this debris re-enters the atmosphere periodically.

Although Earth is the only body within the Solar System known to support life, evidence suggests that in the distant past the planet Mars possessed bodies of liquid water on the surface.[93] For a brief period in Mars' history, it may have also been capable of forming life. At present though, most of the water remaining on Mars is frozen. If life exists at all on Mars, it is most likely to be located underground where liquid water can still exist.[94]

Conditions on the other terrestrial planets, Mercury and Venus, appear to be too harsh to support life as we know it. But it has been conjectured that Europa, the fourth-largest moon of Jupiter, may possess a sub-surface ocean of liquid water and could potentially host life.[95]

Astronomers have started to discover extrasolar Earth analogs – planets that lie in the habitable zone

CHAPTER THREE

In August

As Oasis HD[edit]

In August 2005, John S. Panikkar (co-founder of the channel's original owner, High Fidelity HDTV), was granted a licence by the Canadian Radio-television and Telecommunications Commission (CRTC) to launch OasisHD, described as "a national English-language Category 2 high definition specialty programming undertaking... featuring urban and wild landscapes by Canadian and international cinematographers."[1]

The channel launched in Canada on March 12, 2006, as Oasis HD,[2] focusing on wildlife and nature programming, similar to its current format.

On December 21, 2011, High Fidelity HDTV announced that it had entered into an agreement to be purchased outright by Blue Ant Media. While initially purchasing 29.9% of the company, the remaining 70.1% would be purchased once it is approved by the CRTC.[3]

Logo as Oasis from 2014 to 2015.

In the summer of 2014, the channel dropped the "HD" moniker and was re-branded as Oasis with a revised logo and new website.

On January 19, 2015, Oasis re-branded again, this time as Love Nature. The re-branding coincided with an announcement by Blue Ant Media that it planned to produce 200 hours of nature programming per-year in 4K Ultra HD.[4]

Makeful replaced BiteTV on August 24, 2015 and it became a sister station to Makeful as with other Blue Ant channels.

International expansion[edit]

On July 14, 2008, then owners High Fidelity HDTV, announced that it had reached an agreement with Cameron Thomson Group to distribute then Oasis HD, throughout Europe.[5] Although the channel did not launch internationally as planned.

On December 14, 2015, Blue Ant Media and Smithsonian Networks jointly announced that it was partnering in a new joint venture called Blue Skye Entertainment, with the new company focusing on developing and distributing 4K Ultra HD wildlife and nature programming globally via SVOD and linear television services under the Love Nature brand and Smithsonian Network's stand-alone streaming service, Smithsonian Earth.[6] The new company's first product launch came with the launch of the Love Nature SVOD streaming service, which launched in 32 countries at launch, in February 2016.[7]

The channel's first international linear television distribution agreement was signed with StarHub TV in Singapore in November 2016.[8]

The channel launched on Virgin Media on channels 293 and 294 in the United Kingdom on 21 July 2018.

The channel launched on Ziggo on channel 205 in the Netherlands on 1 February 2019.[9]

The channel launched on MyTV SUPER on channels 402 and 403 in Hong Kong on 11 March 2019, available in

HD and 4K formats.

The channel launched on Unifi TV on channel 502 in Malaysia and channel 746 in the United States on 15 January 2020, available in HD and 4K formats.

The channel launched on AIS Play on channel 505 in Thailand on 1 August 2020, available in HD and 4K formats.

The channel launched on Cignal TV and SkyCable on Channel 203 and Channel 266 in Philippines on February 28 2022 available soon in HD formats.

References

CHAPTER FOUR

compassion,

Love encompasses a range of strong and positive emotional and mental states, from the most sublime virtue or good habit, the deepest interpersonal affection, to the simplest pleasure.[1][2] An example of this range of meanings is that the love of a mother differs from the love of a spouse, which differs from the love for food. Most commonly, love refers to a feeling of a strong attraction and emotional attachment.[3][4][additional citation(s) needed]

Love is considered to be both positive and negative, with its virtue representing human kindness, compassion, and affection, as "the unselfish loyal and benevolent concern for the good of another" and its vice representing human moral flaw, akin to vanity, selfishness, amour-propre, and egotism, as potentially leading people into a type of mania, obsessiveness or codependency.[5][6] It may also describe compassionate and affectionate actions towards other humans, one's self, or animals.[7] In its various forms, love acts as a major facilitator of interpersonal relationships and, owing to its central psychological importance, is one of the most common themes in the creative arts.[8] Love has been postulated to be a function that keeps human beings together against menaces and to facilitate the continuation of the species.[9]

Ancient Greek philosophers identified six forms of love: essentially, familial love (in Greek, Storge), friendly love or platonic love (Philia), romantic love (Eros), self-love (Philautia), guest love (Xenia), and divine love (Agape). Modern authors have distinguished further varieties of love: unrequited love, empty love, companionate love, consummate love, infatuated love, self-love, and courtly love. Numerous cultures have also distinguished Ren, Yuanfen, Mamihlapinatapai, Cafuné, Kama, Bhakti, Mettā, Ishq, Chesed, Amore, Charity, Saudade (and other variants or symbioses of these states), as culturally unique words, definitions, or expressions of love in regards to a specified "moments" currently lacking in the English language.[10][11][12]

Scientific research on emotion has increased significantly over the past two decades. The color wheel theory of love defines three primary, three secondary and nine tertiary love styles, describing them in terms of the traditional color wheel. The triangular theory of love suggests "intimacy, passion and commitment" are core components of love. Love has additional religious or spiritual meaning. This diversity of uses and meanings combined with the complexity of the feelings involved makes love unusually difficult to consistently define, compared to other emotional states.

Romeo and Juliet, depicted as they part on the balcony in Act III, 1867 by Ford Madox Brown

The word "love" can have a variety of related but distinct meanings in different contexts. Many other languages use multiple words to express some of the different concepts that in English are denoted as "love"; one example is the plurality of Greek concepts for "love" (agape, eros, philia, storge) .[13] Cultural differences in conceptualizing love thus doubly impede the establishment of a universal definition.[14]

Although the nature or essence of love is a subject of frequent debate, different aspects of the word can be clarified by determining what isn't love (antonyms of "love"). Love as a general expression of positive sentiment (a stronger form of like) is commonly contrasted with hate (or neutral apathy). As a less-sexual and more-emotionally intimate form of romantic attachment, love is commonly contrasted with lust. As an interpersonal relationship with romantic overtones, love is sometimes contrasted with friendship, although the word love is often applied to close friendships or platonic love. (Further possible ambiguities come with usages "girlfriend", "boyfriend", "just good friends").

Fraternal love (Prehispanic sculpture from 250 to 900 AD, of Huastec origin). Museum of Anthropology in Xalapa, Veracruz, Mexico

Abstractly discussed, love usually refers to an experience one person feels for another. Love often involves caring for, or identifying with, a person or thing (cf. vulnerability and care theory of love), including oneself (cf. narcissism). In addition to cross-cultural differences in understanding love, ideas about love have also changed greatly over time. Some historians date modern conceptions of romantic love to courtly Europe during or after the Middle Ages, although the prior existence of romantic attachments is attested by ancient love poetry.[15]

The complex and abstract nature of love often reduces discourse of love to a thought-terminating cliché. Several common proverbs regard love, from Virgil's "Love conquers all" to The Beatles‘ "All You Need Is Love". St. Thomas Aquinas, following Aristotle, defines love as "to will the good of another."[16] Bertrand Russell describes love as a condition of "absolute value," as opposed to relative value.[citation needed] Philosopher Gottfried Leibniz said that love is "to be delighted by the happiness of another."[17] Meher Baba stated that in love there is a "feeling of unity" and an "active appreciation of the intrinsic worth of the object of love."[18] Biologist Jeremy Griffith defines love as "unconditional selflessness".[19]

Impersonal

People can be said to love an object, principle, or goal to which they are deeply committed and greatly value. For example, compassionate outreach and volunteer workers' "love" of their cause may sometimes be born not of interpersonal love but impersonal love, altruism, and strong spiritual or political convictions.[20] People can also "love" material objects, animals, or activities if they invest themselves in bonding or otherwise identifying with those things. If sexual passion is also involved, then this feeling is called paraphilia.[21]

Interpersonal

e

Interpersonal love refers to love between human beings. It is a much more potent sentiment than a simple liking for a person. Unrequited love refers to those feelings of love that are not reciprocated. Interpersonal love is most closely associated with Interpersonal relationships.[20] Such love might exist between family members, friends, and couples. There are also a number of psychological disorders related to love, such as erotomania. Throughout history, philosophy and religion have done the most speculation on the phenomenon of love. In the 20th century, the science of psychology has written a great deal on the subject. In recent years, the sciences of psychology, anthropology, neuroscience, and biology have added to the understanding of the concept of love.

Biological basis

Main article: Biological basis of love

Biological models of sex tend to view love as a mammalian drive, much like hunger or thirst.[22] Helen Fisher, an anthropologist and human behavior researcher, divides the experience of love into three partly overlapping stages: lust, attraction, and attachment. Lust is the feeling of sexual desire; romantic attraction determines what partners mates find attractive and pursue, conserving time and energy by choosing; and attachment involves sharing a home, parental duties, mutual defense, and in humans involves feelings of safety and security.[23] Three distinct neural circuitries, including neurotransmitters, and three behavioral patterns, are associated with these three romantic styles.[23]

Pair of Lovers. 1480–1485

Lust is the initial passionate sexual desire that promotes mating, and involves the increased release of chemicals such as testosterone and estrogen. These effects rarely last more than a few weeks or months. Attraction is the more individualized and romantic desire for a specific candidate for mating, which develops out of lust as commitment to an individual mate forms. Recent studies in neuroscience have indicated that as people fall in love, the brain consistently releases a certain set of chemicals, including the neurotransmitter hormones, dopamine, norepinephrine, and serotonin, the same compounds released by amphetamine, stimulating the brain's pleasure center and leading to side effects such as increased heart rate, loss of appetite and sleep, and an intense feeling of excitement. Research has indicated that this stage generally lasts from one and a half to three years.[24]

Since the lust and attraction stages are both considered temporary, a third stage is needed to account for long-term relationships. Attachment is the bonding that promotes relationships lasting for many years and even decades. Attachment is generally based on commitments such as marriage and children, or mutual friendship based on things like shared interests. It has been linked to higher levels of the chemicals oxytocin and vasopressin to a greater degree than short-term relationships have.[24] Enzo Emanuele and coworkers reported the protein molecule known as the nerve growth factor (NGF) has high levels when people first fall in love, but these return to previous levels after one year.[25]

Psychological basis

Further information: Human bonding

Grandmother and grandchild in Sri Lanka

Psychology depicts love as a cognitive and social phenomenon. Psychologist Robert Sternberg formulated a triangular theory of love and argued that love has three different components: intimacy, commitment, and passion. Intimacy is a form in which two people share confidences and various details of their personal lives, and is usually shown in friendships and romantic love affairs. Commitment, on the other hand, is the expectation that the relationship is permanent. The last form of love is sexual attraction and passion. Passionate love is shown in infatuation as well as romantic love. All forms of love are viewed as varying combinations of these three components. Non-love does not include any of these components. Liking only includes intimacy. Infatuated love only includes passion. Empty love only includes commitment. Romantic love includes both intimacy and passion. Companionate love includes intimacy and commitment. Fatuous love includes passion and commitment. Lastly, consummate love includes all three components.[26] American psychologist Zick Rubin sought to define love by psychometrics in the 1970s. His work states that three factors constitute love: attachment, caring, and intimacy.[27][28]

Following developments in electrical theories such as Coulomb's law, which showed that positive and negative charges attract, analogs in human life were developed, such as "opposites attract". Over the last century, research on the nature of human mating has generally found this not to be true when it comes to character and personality—people tend to like people similar to themselves. However, in a few unusual and specific domains, such as immune systems, it seems that humans prefer others who are unlike themselves (e.g., with an orthogonal immune system), since this will lead to a baby that has the best of both worlds.[29] In recent years, various human bonding theories have been developed, described in terms of attachments, ties, bonds, and affinities. Some Western authorities disaggregate into two main components, the altruistic and the narcissistic. This view is represented in the works of Scott Peck, whose work in the field of applied psychology explored the definitions of love and evil. Peck maintains that love is a combination of the "concern for the spiritual growth of another," and simple narcissism.[30] In combination, love is an activity, not simply a feeling.

Psychologist Erich Fromm maintained in his book The Art of Loving that love is not merely a feeling but is also actions, and that in fact, the "feeling" of love is superficial in comparison to one's commitment to love via a series of loving actions over time.[20] In this sense, Fromm held that love is ultimately not a feeling at all, but rather is a commitment to, and adherence to, loving actions towards another, oneself, or many others, over a sustained duration.[20] Fromm also described love as a conscious choice that in its early stages might originate as an involuntary feeling, but which then later no longer depends on those feelings, but rather depends only on conscious commitment.[20]

Evolutionary basis

Wall of Love on Montmartre in Paris: "I love you" in 250 languages, by calligraphist Fédéric Baron and artist Claire Kito (2000)

Evolutionary psychology has attempted to provide various reasons for love as a survival tool. Humans are dependent on parental help for a large portion of their lifespans compared to other mammals. Love has therefore been seen as a mechanism to promote parental support of children for this extended time period. Furthermore, researchers as early as Charles Darwin himself identified unique features of human love compared to other mammals and credit love as a major factor for creating social support systems that enabled the development and expansion of the human species.[31] Another factor may be that sexually transmitted diseases can cause, among other effects, permanently reduced fertility, injury to the fetus, and increase complications during childbirth. This would favor monogamous relationships over polygamy.[32]

Adaptive benefit

Interpersonal love between a male and a female is considered to provide an evolutionary adaptive benefit since it facilitates mating and sexual reproduction.[33]

However, some organisms can reproduce asexually without mating. Thus understanding the adaptive benefit of interpersonal love depends on understanding the adaptive benefit of sexual reproduction as opposed to asexual reproduction. Michod[33] has reviewed evidence that love, and consequently sexual reproduction, provides two major adaptive advantages. First, love leading to sexual reproduction facilitates repair of damages in the DNA that is passed from parent to progeny (during meiosis, a key stage of the sexual process). Second, a gene in either parent may contain a harmful mutation, but in the progeny produced by sex reproduction, expression of a harmful mutation introduced by one parent is likely to be masked by expression of the unaffected homologous gene from the other parent.[33]

Comparison of scientific models

Biological models of love tend to see it as a mammalian drive, similar to hunger or thirst.[22] Psychology sees love as more of a social and cultural phenomenon. Certainly, love is influenced by hormones (such as oxytocin), neurotrophins (such as NGF), and pheromones, and how people think and behave in love is influenced by their conceptions of love. The conventional view in biology is that there are two major drives in love: sexual attraction and attachment. Attachment between adults is presumed to work on the same principles that lead an infant to become attached to its mother. The traditional psychological view sees love as being a combination of companionate love and passionate love. Passionate love is intense longing, and is often accompanied by physiological arousal (shortness of breath, rapid heart rate); companionate love is affection and a feeling of intimacy not accompanied by physiological arousal.

Cultural views

Ancient Greek

See also: Greek words for love

Roman copy of a Greek sculpture by Lysippus depicting Eros, the Greek personification of romantic love

Greek distinguishes several different senses in which the word "love" is used. Ancient Greeks identified four forms of love: kinship or familiarity (in Greek, storge), friendship and/or platonic desire (philia), sexual and/or romantic desire (eros), and self-emptying or divine love (agape).[34][35] Modern authors have distinguished further varieties of romantic love.[36] However, with Greek (as with many other languages), it has been historically difficult to separate the meanings of these words totally. At the same time, the Ancient Greek text of the Bible has examples of the verb agapo having the same meaning as phileo.

Agape (ἀγάπη agápē) means love in modern-day Greek. The term s'agapo means I love you in Greek. The word agapo is the verb I love. It generally refers to a "pure," ideal type of love, rather than the physical attraction suggested by eros. However, there are some examples of agape used to mean the same as eros. It has also been translated as "love of the soul."[37]

Eros (ἔρως érōs) (from the Greek deity Eros) is passionate love, with sensual desire and longing. The Greek word erota means in love. Plato refined his own definition. Although eros is initially felt for a person, with contemplation it becomes an appreciation of the beauty within that person, or even becomes appreciation of beauty itself. Eros helps the soul recall knowledge of beauty and contributes to an understanding of spiritual truth. Lovers and philosophers are all inspired to seek truth by eros. Some translations list it as "love of the body".[37]

Philia (φιλία philía), a dispassionate virtuous love, was a concept addressed and developed by Aristotle in his Nicomachean Ethics Book VIII.[38] It includes loyalty to friends, family, and community, and requires virtue, equality, and familiarity. Philia is motivated by practical reasons; one or both of the parties benefit from the relationship. It can also mean "love of the mind."

Storge (στοργή storgē) is natural affection, like that felt by parents for offspring.

Xenia (ξενία xenía), hospitality, was an extremely important practice in ancient Greece. It was an almost ritualized friendship formed between a host and his guest, who could previously have been strangers. The host fed and provided quarters for the guest, who was expected to repay only with gratitude. The importance of this can be seen throughout Greek mythology—in particular, Homer's Iliad and Odyssey.

Ancient Roman (Latin)

The Latin language has several different verbs corresponding to the English word "love." amō is the basic verb meaning I love, with the infinitive amare ("to love") as it still is in Italian today. The Romans used it both in an affectionate sense as well as in a romantic or sexual sense. From this verb come amans—a lover, amator, "professional lover," often with the accessory notion of lechery—and amica, "girlfriend" in the English sense, often being applied euphemistically to a prostitute. The corresponding noun is amor (the significance of this term for the Romans is well illustrated in the fact, that the name of the city, Rome—in Latin: Roma—can be viewed as an anagram for amor, which was used as the secret name of the City in wide circles in ancient times),[39] which is also used in the plural form to indicate love affairs or sexual adventures. This same root also produces amicus—"friend"—and amicitia, "friendship" (often based to mutual advantage, and corresponding sometimes more closely to "indebtedness" or "influence"). Cicero wrote a treatise called On Friendship (de Amicitia), which discusses the notion at some length. Ovid wrote a guide to dating called Ars Amatoria (The Art of Love), which addresses, in depth, everything from extramarital affairs to overprotective parents.

Latin sometimes uses amāre where English would simply say to like. This notion, however, is much more generally expressed in Latin by the terms placere or delectāre, which are used more colloquially, the latter used frequently in the love poetry of Catullus. Diligere often has the notion "to be affectionate for," "to esteem," and rarely if ever is used for romantic love. This word would be appropriate to describe the friendship of two men. The corresponding noun diligentia, however, has the meaning of "diligence" or "carefulness," and has little semantic overlap with the verb. Observare is a synonym for diligere; despite the cognate with English, this verb and its corresponding noun, observantia, often denote "esteem" or "affection." Caritas is used in Latin translations of the Christian Bible to mean "charitable love"; this meaning, however, is not found in Classical pagan Roman literature. As it arises from a conflation with a Greek word, there is no corresponding verb.

Chinese and other Sinic

愛 (Mandarin: ài), the traditional Chinese character for love contains a heart (心) in the middle.

Two philosophical underpinnings of love exist in the Chinese tradition, one from Confucianism which emphasized actions and duty while the other came from Mohism which championed a universal love. A core concept to Confucianism is 仁 (Ren, "benevolent love"), which focuses on duty, action, and attitude in a relationship rather than love itself. In Confucianism, one displays benevolent love by performing actions such as filial piety from children, kindness from parents, loyalty to the king and so forth.

The concept of 愛 (Mandarin: ài) was developed by the Chinese philosopher Mozi in the 4th century BC in reaction to Confucianism's benevolent love. Mozi tried to replace what he considered to be the long-entrenched Chinese over-attachment to family and clan structures with the concept of "universal love" (兼愛, jiān'ài). In this, he argued directly against Confucians who believed that it was natural and correct for people to care about different people in different degrees. Mozi, by contrast, believed people in principle should care for all people equally. Mohism stressed that rather than adopting different attitudes towards different people, love should be unconditional and offered to everyone without regard to reciprocation; not just to friends, family and other Confucian relations. Later in Chinese Buddhism, the term Ai (愛) was adopted to refer to a passionate, caring love and was considered a fundamental desire. In Buddhism, Ai was seen as capable of being either selfish or selfless, the latter being a key element towards enlightenment.

In Mandarin Chinese, 愛 (ài) is often used as the equivalent of the Western concept of love. 愛 (ài) is used as both a verb (e.g. 我愛你, Wǒ ài nǐ, or "I love you") and a noun (such as 愛情 àiqíng, or "romantic love"). However, due to the influence of Confucian 仁 (rén), the phrase 我愛你 (Wǒ ài nǐ, I love you) carries with it a very specific sense of responsibility, commitment and loyalty. Instead of frequently saying "I love you" as in some Western societies, the Chinese are more likely to express feelings of affection in a more casual way. Consequently, "I like you" (我喜欢你, Wǒ xǐhuan nǐ) is a more common way of expressing affection in Mandarin; it is more playful and less serious.[40] This is also true in Japanese (suki da, 好きだ).

Japanese

The Japanese language uses three words to convey the English equivalent of "love". Because "love" covers a wide range of emotions and behavioral phenomena, there are nuances distinguishing the three terms.[41][42] The term ai (愛), which is often associated with maternal love[41] or selfless love,[42] originally referred to beauty and was often used in a religious context. Following the Meiji Restoration 1868, the term became associated with "love" in order to translate Western literature. Prior to Western influence, the term koi (恋 or 孤悲) generally represented romantic love, and was often the subject of the popular Man'yōshū Japanese poetry collection.[41] Koi describes a longing for a member of the opposite sex and is typically interpreted as selfish and wanting.[42] The term's origins come from the concept of lonely solitude as a result of separation from a loved one. Though modern usage of koi focuses on sexual love and infatuation, the Manyō used the term to cover a wider range of situations, including tenderness, benevolence, and material desire.[41] The third term, ren'ai (恋愛), is a more modern construction that combines the kanji characters for both ai and koi, though its usage more closely resembles that of koi in the form of romantic love.[41][42]

Indian

The love stories of the Hindu deities Krishna and Radha have influenced the Indian culture and arts. Above: Radha Madhavam by Raja Ravi Varma.

In contemporary literature, the Sanskrit words for love is "sneha". Other terms such as Priya refers to innocent love, Prema refers to spiritual love, and Kama refers usually to sexual desire.[43][44] However, the term also refers to any sensory enjoyment, emotional attraction and aesthetic pleasure such as from arts, dance, music, painting, sculpture and nature.[45][46]

The concept of kama is found in some of the earliest known verses in Vedas. For example, Book 10 of Rig Veda describes the creation of the universe from nothing by the great heat. There in hymn 129, it states:

कामस्तदग्रे समवर्तताधि मनसो रेतः परथमं यदासीत |
सतो बन्धुमसति निरविन्दन हृदि परतीष्याकवयो मनीषा ||[47]

Thereafter rose Desire in the beginning, Desire the primal seed and germ of Spirit,
Sages who searched with their heart's thought discovered the existent's kinship in the non-existent.

— Rig Veda, ~ 15th century BC[48]

Persian

The children of Adam are limbs of one body
Having been created of one essence.
When the calamity of time afflicts one limb
The other limbs cannot remain at rest.
If you have no sympathy for the troubles of others
You are not worthy to be called by the name of "man".

Sa'di, Gulistan

Rumi, Hafiz,and Sa'di are icons of the passion and love that the Persian culture and language present.[citation needed] The Persian word for love is Ishq, which is derived from Arabic language; however, it is considered by most to be too stalwart a term for interpersonal love and is more commonly substituted for "doost dashtan" ("liking").[citation needed] In the Persian culture, everything is encompassed by love and all is for love, starting from loving friends and family, husbands and wives, and eventually reaching the divine love that is the ultimate goal in life.[citation needed]

Religious views

Main article: Religious views on love

Abrahamic

Robert Indiana's 1977 Love sculpture spelling ahava

Judaism

See also: Jewish views on love

In Hebrew, אהבה (ahava) is the most commonly used term for both interpersonal love and love between God and God's creations. Chesed, often translated as loving-kindness, is used to describe many forms of love between human beings.

The commandment to love other people is given in the Torah, which states, "Love your neighbor like yourself" (Leviticus 19:18). The Torah's commandment to love God "with all your heart, with all your soul and with all your might" (Deuteronomy 6:5) is taken by the Mishnah (a central text of the Jewish oral law) to refer to good deeds, willingness to sacrifice one's life rather than commit certain serious transgressions, willingness to sacrifice all of one's possessions, and being grateful to the Lord despite adversity (tractate Berachoth 9:5). Rabbinic literature differs as to how this love can be developed, e.g., by contemplating divine deeds or witnessing the marvels of nature.

As for love between marital partners, this is deemed an essential ingredient to life: "See life with the wife you love" (Ecclesiastes 9:9). Rabbi David Wolpe writes that "...love is not only about the feelings of the lover...It is when one person believes in another person and shows it." He further states that "...love...is a feeling that expresses itself in action. What we really feel is reflected in what we do."[49] The biblical book Song of Solomon is considered a romantically phrased metaphor of love between God and his people, but in its plain reading, reads like a love song. The 20th-century rabbi Eliyahu Eliezer Dessler is frequently quoted as defining love from the Jewish point of view as "giving without expecting to take" (from his Michtav me-Eliyahu, Vol. 1).

Christianity

Love and not a one-way street in romanticism

The Christian understanding is that love comes from God, who is himself Love (1 Jn 4:8). The love of man and woman—eros in Greek—and the unselfish love of others (agape), are often contrasted as "descending" and "ascending" love, respectively, but are ultimately the same thing.[50]

There are several Greek words for "love" that are regularly referred to in Christian circles.

Agape: In the New Testament, agapē is charitable, selfless, altruistic, and unconditional. It is parental love, seen as creating goodness in the world; it is the way God is seen to love humanity, and it is seen as the kind of love that

Christians aspire to have for one another.[37]

Phileo: Also used in the New Testament, phileo is a human response to something that is found to be delightful. Also known as "brotherly love."

Two other words for love in the Greek language, eros (sexual love) and storge (child-to-parent love), were never used in the New Testament.[37]

Christians believe that to Love God with all your heart, mind, and strength and Love your neighbor as yourself are the two most important things in life (the greatest commandment of the Jewish Torah, according to Jesus; cf. Gospel of Mark chapter 12, verses 28–34). Saint Augustine summarized this when he wrote "Love God, and do as thou wilt."

The Apostle Paul glorified love as the most important virtue of all. Describing love in the famous poetic interpretation in 1 Corinthians, he wrote, "Love is patient, love is kind. It does not envy, it does not boast, it is not proud. It is not rude, it is not self-seeking, it is not easily angered, it keeps no record of wrongs. Love does not delight in evil but rejoices with the truth. It always protects, always trusts, always hopes, and always perseveres." (1 Cor. 13:4–7, NIV)

The Apostle John wrote, "For God so loved the world that he gave his one and only Son, that whoever believes in him shall not perish but have eternal life. For God did not send his Son into the world to condemn the world, but to save the world through him." (John 3:16–17, NIV) John also wrote, "Dear friends, let us love one another for love comes from God. Everyone who loves has been born of God and knows God. Whoever does not love does not know God, because God is love." (1 John 4:7–8, NIV)

Saint Augustine wrote that one must be able to decipher the difference between love and lust. Lust, according to Saint Augustine, is an overindulgence, but to love and be loved is what he has sought for his entire life. He even says, "I was in love with love." Finally, he does fall in love and is loved back, by God. Saint Augustine says the only one who can love you truly and fully is God, because love with a human only allows for flaws such as "jealousy, suspicion, fear, anger, and contention." According to Saint Augustine, to love God is "to attain the peace which is yours." (Saint Augustine's Confessions)

Augustine regards the duplex commandment of love in Matthew 22 as the heart of Christian faith and the interpretation of the Bible. After the review of Christian doctrine, Augustine treats the problem of love in terms of use and enjoyment until the end of Book I of De Doctrina Christiana (1.22.21–1.40.44;).[51]

Christian theologians see God as the source of love, which is mirrored in humans and their own loving relationships. Influential Christian theologian C. S. Lewis wrote a book called The Four Loves. Benedict XVI named his first encyclical God is love. He said that a human being, created in the image of God, who is love, is able to practice love; to give himself to God and others (agape) and by receiving and experiencing God's love in contemplation (eros). This life of love, according to him, is the life of the saints such as Teresa of Calcutta and Mary, the mother of Jesus and is the direction Christians take when they believe that God loves them.[50]

Pope Francis taught that "True love is both loving and letting oneself be loved...what is important in love is not our loving, but allowing ourselves to be loved by God."[52] And so, in the analysis of a Catholic theologian, for Pope

Francis, "the key to love...is not our activity. It is the activity of the greatest, and the source, of all the powers in the universe: God's."[53]

In Christianity the practical definition of love is summarised by Thomas Aquinas, who defined love as "to will the good of another," or to desire for another to succeed.[16] This is an explanation of the Christian need to love others, including their enemies. As Thomas Aquinas explains, Christian love is motivated by the need to see others succeed in life, to be good people.

Regarding love for enemies, Jesus is quoted in the Gospel of Matthew chapter five:

"You have heard that it was said, 'Love your neighbor and hate your enemy.' But I tell you, love your enemies and pray for those who persecute you, that you may be children of your Father in heaven. He causes his sun to rise on the evil and the good, and sends rain on the righteous and the unrighteous. If you love those who love you, what reward will you get? Are not even the tax collectors doing that? And if you greet only your own people, what are you doing more than others? Do not even pagans do that? Be perfect, therefore, as your heavenly Father is perfect." – Matthew 5: 43–48.

Do not forget to love with forgiveness, Christ saved an adulterous woman from those who would stone her. A world of wronged hypocrites needs forgiving love. Mosaic Law would hold Deuteronomy 22:22-24 "If a man is found lying with a woman married to a husband, then both of them shall die—the man that lay with the woman, and the woman; so you shall put away the evil from Israel. If a young woman who is a virgin is betrothed to a husband, and a man finds her in the city and lies with her, then you shall bring them both out to the gate of that city, and you shall stone them to death with stones, the young woman because she did not cry out in the city, and the man because he humbled his neighbor's wife; so you shall put away the evil from among you."[54][circular reference]

Tertullian wrote regarding love for enemies: "Our individual, extraordinary, and perfect goodness consists in loving our enemies. To love one's friends is common practice, to love one's enemies only among Christians."[55]

Islam

In Islam, one of the 99 names of God is Al-Wadūd, which means "The Loving"

Love encompasses the Islamic view of life as universal brotherhood that applies to all who hold faith. Amongst the 99 names of God (Allah), there is the name Al-Wadud, or "the Loving One," which is found in Surah [Quran 11:90] as well as Surah [Quran 85:14]. God is also referenced at the beginning of every chapter in the Qur'an as Ar-Rahman and Ar-Rahim, or the "Most Compassionate" and the "Most Merciful", indicating that nobody is more loving, compassionate and benevolent than God. The Qur'an refers to God as being "full of loving kindness."

The Qur'an exhorts Muslim believers to treat all people, those who have not persecuted them, with birr or "deep kindness" as stated in Surah [Quran 6:8-9]. Birr is also used by the Qur'an in describing the love and kindness that children must show to their parents.

Ishq, or divine love, is the emphasis of Sufism in the Islamic tradition. Practitioners of Sufism believe that love is a projection of the essence of God to the universe. God desires to recognize beauty, and as if one looks at a mirror to see oneself, God "looks" at himself within the dynamics of nature. Since everything is a reflection of God, the school of Sufism practices seeing the beauty inside the apparently ugly. Sufism is often referred to as the religion of love.[56] God in Sufism is referred to in three main terms, which are the Lover, Loved, and Beloved, with the last of these terms being often seen in Sufi poetry. A common viewpoint of Sufism is that through love, humankind can get back to its inherent purity and grace. The saints of Sufism are infamous for being "drunk" due to their love of God; hence, the constant reference to wine in Sufi poetry and music.

Printed by Libri Plureos GmbH in Hamburg,
Germany